What is the Problem of Consciousness?

Materialism, Awareness
& What-it-is-likeness

Neil Paul Cummins

Cranmore Publications

*A catalogue record for this book is available
from the British Library*

ISBN: 978-1-907962-05-9

Published by Cranmore Publications

Reading, England

For Linda

Contents

Preface

In the face of a seemingly intractable mystery there are two possibilities. Firstly, it could be that there is a genuine mystery which humans are incapable of demystifying. Secondly, it could be that a simple change of perspective – a new way of looking at the problem – can dissolve its intractability.

It is my hope, in this book, to help to initiate a change of perspective towards the seemingly intractable mystery which is widely referred to as the 'problem of consciousness'.

Introduction

The 'problem of consciousness' is the problem of accommodating consciousness within a materialistic worldview. This problem is widely seen as the biggest challenge humanity faces as it seeks to gain a 'complete' understanding of both itself and the non-human world. But what exactly is consciousness?

I contend that the 'problem of consciousness' is widely conceived of as the problem of how it is possible that states of 'what-it-is-likeness' can exist in a material world. I propose that it is this conceptualisation of the problem which leads to its seeming intractability.

An alternative conceptualisation is outlined in which there are two distinct problems – the *problem of awareness* and the *problem of 'what-it-is-likeness'*. It is suggested that this alternative conceptualisation demystifies the 'problem of consciousness'.

What is the Problem of Consciousness?

Both in philosophy and psychology "the problem of consciousness" is supposed to be very special... It has to do with the internal or subjective character of experience, paradigmatically sensory experience, and how such a thing can be accommodated in, or even tolerated by, a materialist theory of the mind.[1]

William G. Lycan

---

[1] William G. Lycan, *Consciousness and Experience*, MIT Press, London, 1996, p. 1.

Consciousness is widely regarded as an intractable mystery... By what mysterious power do our material brains generate these additional conscious feelings?[2]

David Papineau

Human consciousness is just about the last surviving mystery.[3]

Daniel Dennett

---

[2] David Papineau, *Thinking about Consciousness*, OUP, Oxford, 2004, pp. 1-2.

[3] Daniel Dennett, *Consciousness Explained*, Little Brown, Boston, 1991, p. 21.

we know that brains are the *de facto* causal basis of consciousness, but we have, it seems, no understanding whatever of how this can be so. It strikes us as miraculous, eerie, even faintly comic... we are cut off by our very cognitive constitution from... [conceptualizing] the psychophysical link. [4]

Colin McGinn

---

[4] Colin McGinn, 'Can we solve the mind-body problem?', *Mind*, 98 (1989), pp. 349-50.

What is the Problem of Consciousness?

Accommodating consciousness within a materialistic worldview is widely seen as the biggest challenge humanity faces as it seeks to gain a 'complete' understanding of both itself and the non-human world. According to Lycan this "problem of consciousness" is "very special"; according to Papineau the problem is widely regarded as an "intractable mystery"; according to Dennett the problem is "just about the last surviving mystery". McGinn goes further and claims that humans are incapable of solving the problem; however, despite this he curiously claims that humans *can* know that brains cause consciousness. Why is the "problem of consciousness" so special and so mysterious? Answering this question requires a clear understanding of what is meant by the term consciousness.

There is a standard contemporary philosophical use of the term consciousness, a use that is revealed in the above quotes. Papineau describes the problem of consciousness as how material brains generate conscious "feelings", whilst Lycan describes the problem as to do with the "subjective character of experience, paradigmatically sensory experience". The standard use is that the term consciousness refers to states that *feel* a certain way, states that have a certain *subjective character*. These states are also widely referred to either as states of 'what-it-is-likeness' or as states of qualitative feeling/qualia. This standard use of the term consciousness is also clear in the following assertions made by David Chalmers, John Searle and Galen Strawson:

> We can say that a being is conscious if there is *something it is like* to be that being.[5]

> It is a remarkable fact about consciousness... that there is a qualitative feel to any conscious state.[6]

---

[5] David Chalmers, *The Conscious Mind*, OUP, Oxford, 1996, p. 4.

[6] John Searle, *Conversations on Consciousness*, OUP, Oxford, 2005, p. 202.

'consciousness', conscious experience, 'phenomenology', experiential 'what-it's likeness',
feeling, sensation, explicit conscious thought
as we have it and know it at almost every
waking moment. Many words are used to
denote this necessarily occurrent (essentially
non-dispositional) phenomenon, and I will
use the terms 'experience', 'experiential
phenomena' and 'experientiality' to refer to
it.[7]

---

[7] Galen Strawson, *Consciousness and its place in nature*, Imprint Academic, Exeter, 2006, p. 3.

So, despite the use of slightly different terminology – "something it is like", "feeling", "qualitative feel", "experiential 'what-it's likeness'", "subjective character of experience", "phenomenology" – it is clear that the "problem of consciousness" is widely taken to be the problem of how it is possible that states that feel a certain way can exist in a material world; for simplicity I will use just one term 'what-it-is-likeness' to refer to these states. So, the "problem of consciousness" on the standard contemporary view is the *problem of 'what-it-is-likeness'*. That this is so should already be clear, but let us also consider how McGinn describes the "problem of consciousness":

We have a good idea how the Big Bang led to the creation of stars and galaxies, principally by the force of gravity. But we know of no comparable force that might explain how ever-expanding lumps of matter might have developed an inner conscious life.[8]

consciousness... the having of sensations, emotions, feelings, thoughts.[9]

---

[8] Colin McGinn, *The Mysterious Flame*, Basic Books, New York, 1999, p. 15.

[9] Colin McGinn, *The Mysterious Flame*, Basic Books, New York, 1999, pp. 2-3.

So, according to McGinn, the "problem of consciousness" is that we have no idea what the "force" is that could cause matter to "develop an inner conscious life". And according to McGinn the term consciousness means sensations, emotions, feelings and thoughts. This is, of course, essentially the same use of the term as we have already encountered. So, whilst McGinn uses the term to refer to a diverse array of phenomena (sensations, emotions, feelings and thoughts) there is assumed to be a common thread linking all of these phenomena – they are states of the world that feel a certain way; that is, they are states of the world that have 'what-it-is-likeness'. This means that McGinn also takes the "problem of consciousness" to be the problem of how it is possible for states of 'what-it-is-likeness' to exist in a material world.

What have we concluded so far? We have concluded that the "problem of consciousness" is widely conceived of as the problem of how it is possible for states of 'what-it-is-likeness' to exist in a material world. This means that if the universe was wholly comprised of states of *'nothing-it-is-likeness'* (which, of course, it is not) then, it would seem that according to this view there would be no "problem of consciousness" in need of a solution. In other words, it is the *mere existence* of states of 'what-it-is-likeness' that generates the "problem of conscious-ness"; why particular material states are (or are associated with) particular 'what-it-is-likeness'

21

states is a separate issue. In short, if one is a materialist *and* one asserts that there was a time when the material world was wholly devoid of 'what-it-is-likeness' then one faces the "very special" problem of having to explain how that world evolves 'what-it-is-likeness'. According to the standard contemporary view this problem *is* the "problem of consciousness".

An implication of the standard contemporary view is that if one were to suppose that the entire material world is, and always has been, pervaded by states of 'what-it-is-likeness' (let us call this position 'panwhat-it-is-likeness') then the "problem of consciousness" would no longer exist. This will surely strike one as implausible. To be clear, it is not 'panwhat-it-is-likeness' which is implausible, it is the implication that if 'panwhat-it-is-likeness' is true that there is no "problem of consciousness" which is implausible. What exactly does 'panwhat-it-is-likeness' entail? It simply entails the assertion that the entire material world is pervaded by 'what-it-is-likeness' – that when two stones collide, and when a raindrop hits the ocean, that states of qualitative feeling are generated. There is clearly no entailment that these states of 'what-it-is-likeness' involve awareness. A 'panwhat-it-is-likeness' world could be wholly devoid of awareness.

According to the standard contemporary view the "problem of consciousness" *is* the problem of 'what-it-is-likeness'. Now, of course, the advocates of the standard contemporary view do take themselves to be giving an account of awareness, this is because they implicitly assume that to talk of 'what-it-is-likeness' *is* to talk of awareness. That is – they assume that if there is a state of awareness that this state *itself* feels a certain way; contrarily, they assume that if there is a state that feels a certain way that this state *itself* must be a state of awareness. On this view, if one has an account of 'what-it-is-likeness' then one also has an account of awareness.

Now, if it is intelligible, which it surely is, for there to be a 'panwhat-it-is-likeness' world which is wholly devoid of awareness, then this means that the "problem of consciousness" is actually two distinct problems – the *problem of 'what-it-is-likeness'* and the *problem of awareness*. In conflating the two problems the standard contemporary view takes itself to be addressing the *problem of awareness* by addressing the *problem of 'what-it-is-likeness'*. However, if there are actually two problems then this is clearly inappropriate. For, the 'panwhat-it-is-likeness' advocate does not face the *problem of 'what-it-is-likeness'* but they still face the *problem of awareness*. When the *problem of 'what-it-is-likeness'* is solved the "problem of consciousness" can remain unsolved.

What exactly is the *problem of awareness*? As a first insight into the nature of this problem we can consider the following passage from Iris Murdoch's *The Black Prince*:

Angels must wonder at these beings who fall so regularly out of awareness into a fantasm-infested dark. How our frail identities survive these chasms no philosopher has ever been able to explain.[10]

Now, the beings in question are clearly human beings, and our current interest is not the existence of human personal identity through time, it is the related issue of such identities being "frail" because we are beings who "fall so regularly out of aware-ness" into "chasms" of darkness. In short, humans are parts of the world which oscillate between

[10] Iris Murdoch, *The Black Prince*, Penguin Books, London, 1973, p. 224.

having awareness of the world and losing awareness of the world. Of course, there will be some people who deny this, but to the overwhelming majority of people it is surely an obvious fact that they, as humans, oscillate between having awareness of the world and losing awareness of the world. Not only does this seem to be an obvious fact, it is also one of the most fundamental aspects of human existence. At a particular time after being forged from a zygote a human first becomes aware of the world. Then at a future time this awareness is lost as the human enters a state that perhaps can be labelled an 'unconscious' state, most probably a particular type of 'unconscious' state which can be labelled a 'sleep' state. From this moment on the rest of a human life is shaped around the seemingly obvious fact that a human repeatedly oscillates between states of awareness of the world and states where this awareness is lacking. The life of a human ends when this oscillation cycle ceases, when an 'unconscious' state is entered from which the human never returns.

If one accepts that awareness of the world is something which has evolved – that if one goes far enough back in time that the entire universe was wholly devoid of awareness – then clearly one faces the *problem of awareness*. This is the problem of explaining how it is possible that a material world which is devoid of awareness can evolve awareness. Of course, there are those who believe that the entire material world is pervaded by states of awareness, and that it always has been pervaded by such states; clearly, if one were to adopt this view then one would not face the *problem of awareness*; let us refer to this view as 'panawareness'. The advocate of panwhat-it-is-likeness believes that when two stones collide this involves states of 'what-it-is-likeness' but that it does not involve states of awareness. Contrarily, the advocate of panawareness believes that this interaction involves both states of 'what-it-is-likeness' and states of awareness (the motivation for adopting panawareness is that one does not need to resort to unknown 'forces' in order to explain the emergence of awareness, the panawareness advocate will therefore also hold that 'what-it-is-likeness' is a non-emergent pervasive phenomenon). This means that the panawareness view is in opposition to both the standard contemporary view and panwhat-it-is-likeness. For according to both of these views awareness is a state of the world which evolves; it is just that the standard contemporary view asserts that this evolutionary event is simultaneously the evolution of 'what-it-is-likeness', whilst the panwhat-it-is-likeness advocate denies that this is so.

In order to appreciate the differences between these three views – the standard contemporary view, panwhat-it-is-likeness, and panawareness – it is useful to consider a human who is in an 'uncon-scious' state; in this state it is *a seemingly obvious fact* that the human has no awareness of the world. According to the standard contemporary view a human in this state is devoid of 'what-it-is-likeness'/awareness. According to the panwhat-it-is-likeness advocate a human in this state is devoid of awareness but contains states of 'what-it-is-likeness'. This means that both of these views accord with the *seemingly obvious fact*. Contrarily, the panawareness advocate believes that a human in the 'unconscious' state has states of awareness of the world and thereby rejects the *seemingly obvious fact*. If the *seemingly obvious fact* is one of the most fundamental aspects of human existence, which it seems to be, then there would need to be a very good reason to adopt a theory which rejects it.

So, what *is* the "problem of consciousness"? According to the standard contemporary view it is the problem of explaining how states of 'what-it-is-likeness'/awareness evolve in a material world. According to the panwhat-it-is-likeness advocate it is the problem of explaining how states of awareness evolve in a (panwhat-it-is-likeness) material world. According to the panawareness advocate there is no "problem of consciousness"; the problem with this view being that it rejects the *seemingly obvious fact*. If one accepts the truth of the *seemingly obvious fact* then there is a "problem of consciousness" to be solved. It is either the *problem of awareness* or the *problem of 'what-it-is-likeness'/awareness*.

There is clearly a strong case for adopting a panwhat-it-is-likeness view of the material world. For this view fully naturalises 'what-it-is-likeness' and takes much of the mystery out of the "problem of consciousness". It is only if one believes that the material world is largely devoid of 'what-it-is-likeness' that the "problem of consciousness" is "miraculous" (McGinn) and "very special" (Lycan).

The *problem of consciousness* still needs to be addressed. However, this problem is not particularly miraculous or special if one adopts a panwhat-it-is-likeness view of the world – it is simply the 'problem of awareness'.

Other books by the author:

Is the Human Species Special? : Why human-induced global warming could be in the interests of life

Should I be a Vegetarian? : A personal reflection on meat-eating, vegetarianism and veganism

How Much of Man is Natural? : Two versions of the international prize-winning essay

The Purpose of the Environmental Crisis : *A Reinterpretation of Hölderlin's Philosophy*

www.ingramcontent.com/pod-product-compliance
Lightning Source LLC
Chambersburg PA
CBHW071801020426
42331CB00008B/2364